Crabapples

Frogs and Toads

Bobbie Kalman & Tammy Everts

🌴 Crabtree Publishing Company

Crabapples

created by bobbie kalman

for Natalie and Bill

Editor-in-Chief
Bobbie Kalman

Writing team
Bobbie Kalman
Tammy Everts

Managing editor
Lynda Hale

Editors
Petrina Gentile
Janine Schaub

Computer design
Lynda Hale
David Schimpky

Color separations and film
Dot 'n Line Image Inc.

Printer
Worzalla Publishing Company

Illustrations
Barb Bedell

Photographs
David G. Barker/Tom Stack & Associates:
    pages 27 (bottom), 28 (bottom)
John Cancalosi/Tom Stack & Associates:
    pages 28 (top), 29 (bottom)
Cincinnati Zoo: pages 18, 27 (top right)
Cristopher Crowley/Tom Stack & Associates: page 22
David M. Dennis/Tom Stack & Associates: page 5
John Gerlach/Tom Stack & Associates: page 8-9
James Kamstra: pages 11 (bottom left), 25, 30
Diane Payton Majumdar: pages 13, 19 (top)
Joe McDonald/Joe McDonald Wildlife Photography: title page,
    pages 4, 6, 7, 10, 11 (top left), 15 (bottom right and left), 16,
    17, 27 (top left), 29 (top)
Joe McDonald/Tom Stack & Associates: cover, pages 14 (left), 24
Joe McDonald/Visuals Unlimited: page 12
Rod Planck/Tom Stack & Associates: pages 19 (bottom), 20-21
Kevin Schafer/Tom Stack & Associates: page 11 (right)
John Shaw/Tom Stack & Associates: page 14 (right)
Robert Tymstra: pages 15 (top), 23, 26

Crabtree Publishing Company

350 Fifth Avenue	360 York Road, RR 4	73 Lime Walk
Suite 3308	Niagara-on-the-Lake	Headington
New York	Ontario, Canada	Oxford OX3 7AD
N.Y. 10118	L0S 1J0	United Kingdom

Cataloging in Publication Data
Kalman, Bobbie, 1947-
    Frogs and toads

(Crabapples)
Includes index.

ISBN 0-86505-615-3 (library bound)   ISBN 0-86505-715-X (pbk.)
The topics covered in this book include the behavior, life cycle, and anatomy of frogs and toads.

1. Frogs - Juvenile literature. 2. Toads - Juvenile literature.
I. Everts, Tammy, 1970-   . II. Title. III. Series: Kalman, Bobbie, 1947-   . Crabapples.

QL668.E2K35 1994   j597.8   LC 94-27535
                                          CIP

What is in this book?

In and out of water

Frogs and toads belong to a group of animals called **amphibians**. An amphibian is an animal that can live on land and in the water.

Most amphibians spend the first part of their lives swimming like fish. As adults they can move about on land, so they spend less time in the water.

Adult amphibians breathe with lungs. They also breathe through their skin.

Amphibians are **cold blooded**. Their body temperature does not always stay the same, as ours does. They are as warm or cold as the air around them.

What is a frog?

Frogs and toads look similar, but they are different in some ways. A frog has smooth, moist skin. It needs to live close to water. If a frog's skin dries out, the frog will die.

Frogs have small teeth on their upper jaw. They do not use their teeth for biting or chewing. They use them for holding prey. Toads do not have teeth.

The long, powerful back legs of frogs allow them to take huge leaps. A frog's back leg has four joints. There is one at the hip, one at the knee, and two at the ankle.

Some tree frogs leap great distances from tree to tree. Sticky disks on the ends of their toes help them land on branches and leaves. The webbed feet of this flying frog help it soar through the air!

What is a toad?

Toads have dry, rough skin. Some toads have lumps on their skin. These lumps are called **tubercles**, or warts.

People once believed that touching a toad would give them warts, but now we know this is not true. A toad's poisonous skin, however, can make animals sick!

Toads can be found far from water. A toad travels by walking, taking short hops, or running on its four legs. Its legs are not as long or strong as a frog's.

Frogs and toads live almost everywhere in the world, except where it is very cold. They stay in cool, shady places when they are hot. They sit in the sun when they are cold.

Some frogs and toads live in holes in the ground. Some live in ponds and lakes. Some live inside flowers or rotting logs. Some even live high up in trees!

11

Yummy frog food!

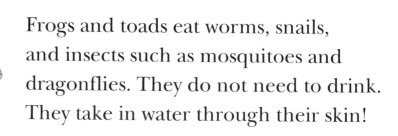

Frogs and toads eat worms, snails, and insects such as mosquitoes and dragonflies. They do not need to drink. They take in water through their skin!

Many frogs and toads have a long, sticky tongue for catching food. The tongue is attached at the front of the mouth. It stays rolled up until it is needed.

When an insect buzzes by, the tongue quickly shoots out, catches the insect, and pulls it into the mouth. Frogs and toads have great aim!

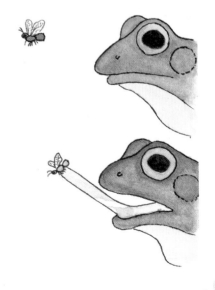

The cycle of life

In the spring and summer, frogs and toads gather in large groups in ponds and streams. These large groups are called **breeding choruses**. They meet to mate and lay eggs. The eggs grow into adult frogs and toads. The changing and growing from egg to adult is called **metamorphosis**. These pictures show the metamorphosis of a frog.

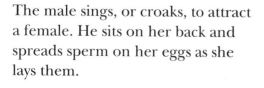

The male sings, or croaks, to attract a female. He sits on her back and spreads sperm on her eggs as she lays them.

1

Females lay hundreds or thousands of eggs in the water. Frogs lay their eggs in clumps. Toads lay them in strings. The eggs are called **spawn**.

4

One day, an adult frog hops out of the water and onto the land. An adult frog's skin does not grow as the frog grows. Instead, the old skin splits and peels off, leaving a brand new skin underneath. Then the frog or toad eats its old skin!

2

After a few days, an egg turns into a **tadpole**. Tadpoles have long tails and breathe through flaps called **gills**. They cannot live out of the water.

3

The tadpoles soon grow legs. They lose their gills and develop lungs for breathing out of water. Their tails get shorter and shorter until they disappear.

15

Ribbit! Ribbit!

Have you ever heard the croaking of frogs and toads on a quiet summer night? Long ago, frogs and toads were the only animals that could make sounds. Now, male and female frogs use sounds to find a mate. Only the males croak, or "sing." The females have quieter voices.

Male frogs and toads sing without opening their mouths! They have a **voice sac** in their throat. The voice sac is made of stretchy skin that swells like a balloon. Inside the balloon of skin, air moves back and forth and echoes. As the air touches the **vocal cords**, it makes a croaking noise.

Some frogs and toads make unusual
sounds. The pig frog sounds like a
grunting pig. The cricket frog sounds
like a chirping cricket. Can you guess
what sound this barking tree frog makes?

Big, bulging eyes

Some frogs and toads have beautiful eyes that come in brilliant colors. Some eyes look like gold or silver. Others look like jewels of red, blue, or green.

A frog or toad's eyes are wide apart, and they bulge from the top of the head. The frog or toad can see above, beside, ahead, and even behind itself to look for food or enemies.

Frogs and toads see well at night. They are also good at seeing moving things. A fly can sit in front of a frog's nose, and the frog will not notice it, but if the fly moves, the frog will eat it in a flash!

Frogs and toads have an extra eyelid. They can see through this clear eyelid. It covers their eyes like a diver's mask when they are swimming.

Eardrums!

Look for the ears on this frog. Believe it or not, almost all frogs and toads have ears! Their ears are very different from the ears of other animals. Frog and toad ears are called **tympanums**.

The tympanum is a thin layer of skin. It does not stick out from the head, and there is no hole. Sound bounces off the tympanum in the same way a drumstick hits a drum. The frog "hears" by feeling the bounce. Male frogs have larger tympanums than female frogs. Frogs have larger tympanums than toads.

Winter sleep

Frogs and toads are cold blooded. They can die of heat during hot weather. They can freeze to death in cold weather. In the winter, frogs and toads must find warm homes to stay alive.

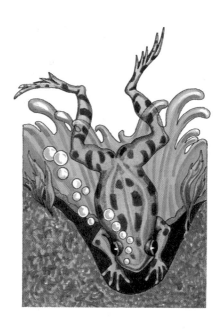

Frogs and toads sleep, or **hibernate**, through the winter. A frog dives down to the bottom of a pond and buries itself in mud. A toad buries itself in the earth or curls up inside a rotting log.

In springtime, the rain softens the
ground and warms up the pond. As the
frog or toad feels the heat, it wakes up
and comes out to enjoy the sunshine.

Safe colors

Frogs and toads have many **predators**. A predator is an animal or bird that hunts and eats another animal. Frogs and toads try to avoid predators such as snakes, otters, and birds, by not being seen. The colors of some frogs and toads allow them to blend into their surroundings.

A frog's green skin is hidden, or **camouflaged**, in greenish pond water or among leaves and grass. When a toad sits on earth, twigs, or dead leaves, its bumpy brown skin is also hard to see.

Deadly colors!

Brightly colored skin shows animals that some frogs and toads are poisonous. A bird might eat a colorful frog such as this poison dart frog and become very sick. That bird would learn never to eat a poison dart frog again!

The poisonous red-bellied tree frog shows off its bright tummy.

The poison dart frog's bright colors warn enemies not to even try eating it!

This friendly looking yellow-headed tree frog makes a nasty-tasting treat for birds and snakes!

Weird frogs

Frogs and toads are fascinating creatures, but some are more interesting than others. Look at the unusual frogs on these pages!

The banjo frog likes to burrow in the sand, where it is protected from enemies and the hot sun.

Watch out! The horned frog below has very sharp teeth and a bad temper.

These tree frogs have long fingers with
sticky tips that help them climb trees.

The casque-headed frog has big, buggy
eyes and a most unusual nose!

No more golden toads!

Frogs and toads are important. They eat harmful insects that could destroy crops or carry diseases. Unfortunately, there are fewer frogs and toads than there used to be. Some people think the reason is that houses and factories have been built where frogs and toads used to live. Other people think that water pollution has killed most of the frogs and toads.

The beautiful golden toads on this page may already be **extinct**. Extinct means that a plant or animal no longer exists. No one has seen a golden toad in several years. Scientists are sorry that they did not have more time to learn about this fabulous toad.

Words to know

amphibian An animal that can live on land and in water

breeding chorus A large group of frogs or toads that gather together to mate

camouflage Patterns or colors that blend into the environment

cold-blooded Describing a body temperature that changes with the weather

extinct Describing plants or animals that no longer exist

gill An opening on the side of the body used for breathing under water

hibernate A long winter sleep

metamorphosis The changes and growth of frogs from egg to adult

predator An animal that eats other animals

spawn The eggs of frogs and toads

tympanum A large, flat, outer eardrum

vocal cord The part of the throat that makes sounds

Index

What is in the picture?

Here is more information about the photographs in this book.

1 2 3 4 5 6 7 8 9 0   Printed in USA   3 2 1 0 9 8 7 6 5 4